I Want To Dance
&
Other Poems

by
Tanure Ojaide

San Francisco	Lagos
African Heritage Press P.O.Box 170613 San Francisco,CA 94117 Phone:415-4698676 E-mail afroheritage9760@aol.com URL:WWW.africanheritagepress.com	23 Unity Road Ikeja Lagos, Nigeria Phone: 234-1-4972044, 080-33128151. E-mail: infoplan2000@yahoo.com

Copyright ©2003 Tanure Ojaide
All rights reserved

No part of this publication may be reproduced or transmitted in any form or by any means, electronic or mechanical, without permission in writing from the publisher.

Library of congress catalog Number:2002115498.

©Cover Design: Dr.Bruce Onobrakpeya,
[selections: 2003]

I WANT TO DANCE & OTHER POEMS.

Poetry, African Studies, African American studies, Cultural studies, and world Literature.

ISBN 0-9628864-5-9

> Owhorakpo je ya vwerie,
> sievo k'ota r'unu-u.
>
> *(Humans branch here and there,
> and so do words of the mouth.)*

Memerume, udje poet and performer of Edjophe in Nigeria's Delta State.

Contents

Preface

1

Daily Worship
My Company
Eastward-bound
I String the Kora
A Bird's Tale
To the Bird of the East
You Will Appear
The Suitor Is Dancing
Swimmer
Moon Phase
To My Realist Friend
Airspace
Healing Song
Island Residence
Roaming the Lightscape
You Defy Capture
Ten Pieces
Birdsong

2

Following the Minstrel's Trail
Many Lives
My Father's Eyes
Blues
Entering the New Millennium

I Want to Dance
Four Pieces
In the Water World
The Apprentice
Reflections
Three Mami Wata Poems
To My Feminist Friend
A Child Holds the Lamp
Guest of the Forest
Signaling Drums
Tobi
Anthill Residence
Night

3

From This Soil That Hurts
Women Writing Africa, in Fez
Jack London
Walla Walla
The Size of Manhood
More Italian Than Catholic
Rivera's Brush
Santa Maria
Discovering Lands
The Liar
Desert Night Shuttle
Awaiting Sentence
The Open Spaces of My Life
Eyes
When the Migrant Returns Home

Glossary

Preface

This spell is yet another phase in the endless song of life. With me, specific times and places evoke certain responses in feelings and ideas that I try to express artistically before they lose their heat. Once Aridon, muse and god of memory, possesses one, there is compulsive grip of the hand to record what is literally frothing in the head and heart. The possessed one becomes restless. At that time nothing else matters until the spell runs out; that is, after the poet has put down what he or she has witnessed personally. Of course, the gift of the god comes with a price—the poet has to present it to the world in a creatively attractive manner, and that demands labour. Most of these poems were written in 2000-2001 in Nigeria, the United States, and during and after travels. Wherever the poet finds himself, the god of songs gives him cause to sing.

I Want to Dance is an individualized metaphor of the human condition. The collection is a song in three segments. There is movement from one emotional state to another in a journey that sometimes takes from west to east and at other times from night through dawn to day. And there is also movement out of and back home. Thus, while the first section generates a surreal and mystical atmosphere, the second section deals with practical experiences and their fresh memories. So, in the opening poems, recurring images of bird, moon, stars, sun, ocean, river, plants, and others symbolize the natural and supernatural dimensions of the quest. The vigil denotes expectation of the arrival of dawn, a bridal face that is a kind of epiphany. The bird becomes, for the poet, both bride and sea-goddess indicative of beauty, love, and fulfillment in various manifestations. The quest thus has its spiritual importance.

By the second group of poems, the quester, a griot/minstrel, paints his observations and experiences on a transparent canvas. The return to a physical level signifies a specific grounding of experiences, different from the earlier phase. The exploration here reflects another type of journey. Local myths

and symbols portray personal experiences, which involve instances of fear, agony, and joy in different endeavors.

The third section relates to memories of the poet's travels. One travel is imagined because it is appropriated from another artist. The travels, as to the Red Sea, Italy, Mexico, Morocco, Baghdad, Jerusalem, and Santa Maria, assume symbolic importance and evoke historical and social events at "home." The physical journeys throw the imagination back to the quest of the first section.

In this journey of triple dimension, the farther I travel, the closer I come home. Movement from the surreal and mystical to the human and physical is one long stream of inspiration that the poet immerses himself to come out and share with others his song of experience.

> To the best
> of my dreams
> I will sing

Edward Kamau Brathwaite, **Arrivants**

Daily Worship

A bird flies into the open house of words
where I am cloistered by command of the caste.
I who daily dance the mask decked with feathers
raise arms to embrace the messenger from afar—
the bird wants for a nest the swaggering tower
I carry on the head and perches for the season.
In the town's gathering place I will have
to open the gift that Aridon wrapped for me,
delivered by the bird become companion.
To the bird that raises the song I sing
I first give abundance before I ever taste
of the sweet berries that fall into my lot.

***

Enter the sun that warms my dance
with the mask of a bird flapping arms.
Come and worship with me.

(February 7, 2001)

My Company

I keep company of two, with whom I light
a bonfire that opens up another world
in which the glowing moon embraces us.
The Delta waters the Sahel—the hurricane
badges in to welcome the harmattan;
butterflies copulate with fireflies
& infidels chant alleluia at dawn of holidays.

On my palms they place a bird of wondrous
plumes and notes. I know how it feels to be caged,
so I stroke my darling and release it into the air—
its freedom elates us all. On its very own,
the bird flies back, only to leave, and return.

It hurts that I can't keep the beauty overnight—
Aridon is ever restless and promises to return,
the angel must report at home for the night.
My companions are loyal to a point on the clock
& alone now I sing snatches of the endless song.

Eastward-Bound

At night I prepare to set out on a journey.
I want to visit her whose face I have not seen—
I should arrive at sunrise when the veil falls off.
I learn that on the route they offer mouthful slices
of coconut cake at the evacuated toll bridge.
A trip of several hours, I prepare for weeks and months—
I sleep over travel plans to put together all I will need.
The clock I reset for departure time has stopped working.
The moon is waiting outside in glistening linen.
Things that should be around are missing or out of order.
Still, I want to pick all that I need for the journey.
I want to visit her mantled in the mist of the east.

(January 24, 2001)

I String The Kora

I

I string the *kora*
to serenade the moon
from first appearance to fullness,
I clear the throat with alligator pepper
for the praise chant of the muse—
I want to wake the world with cannonade
to behold her crowned with moonlight.

II

I wait, far-easterner, for the sun to return
without fail with its ball of heartwarming fire,
I wait for the sunbird to dip into the ocean
and come out with brighter plumes than ever.
Pilgrim that beckons on the wagoner, I am
still handicapped by a capricious tongue—
I will ride in your wheels of light
until shadow gives way to body,
till a face rounds off bridal contours.

I know you have a round face—
I see through the chasm eyes open and close,
I see a mouth laurelled with smiles,
a nose peaked by divine craft;
I see through mountains the cheeks
and hair I seek to touch with reverence.
The aroma divines the tasteful dish!

III

The vine wishes to wrap around the tree
in the evergreen landscape of the forest.
But oh, the east is still wary of giving ears
to the possessed chants of the wanderer;
the bird reaches for reason to warm up
to the compliments rocking the skies.
The brew now ferments in the head
& I know not how far in the sky
it will carry me—Ananse, bless
the singer with a banquet of flavours.

IV

The seeker will surely find the hidden gift—
he chooses where to pray and sing alleluia
because he so loves the blue of the sea
that fills the song with waves and whistles.
He murmurs to the heights a name
he holds fast to his hairy chest,
he looks out to the vast horizon
for the mist-draped one to light up.
His intent lives deep in undercurrents.

v

And the wonders of the vigil come in a vision:
the sun sets and rises in the eyes of the wanderer
who tears through woods and clearings of distance.
He seeks what will keep him always awake, dreaming.
He cares not if the world laughs at his tall encounters
or brands him mad for what he seeks and knows not.
And so he fords night to the eastern shoreline, half-
drowns from the turbulence and depth of daylight
to keep a tryst with the muse, a bird of surreal stock.
Now he promenades dirt paths and alleyways
to the chamber from which the sun always rises
to hug his love in the thick mist of glaring eyes.
The world swarms with birds, but none compares
with plumes and notes of the bird nesting
in the crowned loft of the east. How many
beads of colour can match the fire of diamond?

(December 2, 2000)

A Bird's Tale

I

Listen to the tall-tale fate of the song!
The mist dissolves, the face appears.
It is a bird with a bright tail—
its tongue is deep in flavours,
the feathers rich in colours;
songs and colours it has in abundance.

The bird perches now in my hands,
then takes off into the wilds—
it thrills even as it bites hard.
It tells a tale of tall happenings,
sings to dancing leaves and grass.

My muse is a bird of proud plumes
and deep voice of flavours—
it perches nowhere pedestrian
and nobody can shoot it down.

II

This year a river sprang up
in my backyard. I started
a garden to grow eggs—so
smooth and round when ripe.
A bird helped in the harvest.

River bird
singing from a reed in the tide,
your tenuous hold deters not
the voice from a passionate ring.
I laud your courage for fearing
neither suppliant reed nor tide
about to sweep off your feet,
stilts with which you hop around.
Your song will outlive a fickle fate.

III

Memory bird stares from a tall tree,
stares through horizons of past and future
with stretches of clearings and full growth.

In a year of floods, we indulged our appetites.
We, fishermen, wiped out the farmers' tears—
one family, the festival of songs went on.
A bird from the east sang in boatloads to berth,
it brought multiple births of praise-songs.
The waters will always provide our needs.

Now my bird won't open its mouth,
                              except to sing.
The bell will ring only to summon!

IV

I cursed witches until one captured me.
Her esoteric song's rhythm intensifies
a current of flavours and colours.
The witch flies me into secret places—
my song has crossed many frontiers;
day turns black and nudges night to glow.
A witch remembers her body, so lovely
after soft-landing from blinding stars.
I used to curse witches, but now
the breasts of one do not hurt my tongue.

V

In the morning a bird by the shore
looks at the ocean in the rising sun.
The waves dance in, breaking out.
The bird beats its wings, summons
the spirit of the deep water
& takes off into the skies to sing
above waves and beach-mongers.

VI

Owena has carved me a bird—
it carries a fish in its mouth.
I have danced in the masquerade of birds,
I have told the tale of tall-treed birds.
Will the bird, my muse, be so jealous
of untold memories as not to fly ashore
to be misted in dawn's swathing waves?

VII

A divining bird sits on the crown of a baobab
that looks down on Abuja—of course,
the Assembly curses it: crazy, blind dim-wit.
It nods its white head, clicks its beak—
there are tears pouring out of its throat,
sweat washing off its rainbow costume;
the plumes are wilting from its body
& the wind is plucking quite a number.
"Abuja is bloated with looted oil and gas,
a shameful ring to the nation's anthem."
But the lawmakers curse the divining bird:
crazy, blind dim-wit of no civic learning.
Of course, the Assembly cannot read its fate.

VIII

Even if the homeboy gets his needs around,
he will still not be filled. What a vile curse!
So, from afar in the east the call comes—
the mad chase to relieve the soul begins.
He falls in love with the full moon.
He begins the hunt with a catapult,
bruises feet over thorns and stumps.
He hurls clubs and stones at every brush
to drive out the game he doesn't want to hurt.
The bird calls from the labyrinth of silence.
The moon muse and bird from afar
inflict on him insomniac dreams,
shower him with streams of songs
to light the terrible space between.

(Lagos-Jos-Warri. December 11-21, 2000)

To The Bird Of The East

I

The fruit is ripening over a full moon
& there's hunger harrowing the mouth—
the fasting season is just beginning.

The livery of light grazes night, a clearing
of eggplants sought for their smooth skin.

The stars advance to close our eyes
& are shooting at each other—
there will be no cover from the fire.

I do not see you, but foresee
blooming from the bloodstream
the only flower of its brilliant kind.

I inhale the aroma of your smile
not mellowed by continents between—
I write you in a secret alphabet.

The fruit is ripening to words of faith
as the fasting falters before a fruitcake.

***

After the bird of the east
sang me "Sleep well,"
at day's end I'm a child
rocked by silky arms.
O sun that always rises
a half-world brighter
from my night, bring me
voice, arms and face
in a nest of full moon.

II

Humming a tune,
the herbalist passes
plant after plant;
humming a tune,
he trudges on and on
until his eyes fall
upon what he seeks
& humming a tune,
he plucks the find
into his formula
of a miracle cure.

***

Distance plays truant, plants a wilderness
of poisonous mushrooms between avid palates;
but gleaming through latitudes of horizons, a smile
whose foretaste rallies the song into a possessed chant.

And so the faraway fruit hangs in the air.
Is it still, only a deft stroke of imagination
or inimitable fiber and savour to live on?

You Will Appear

You will appear
at the end of the long road
cutting across chasms—
for a moment light will stand still
to recount bright memories
that threaten future solace.
I will see you at daylight
where the road meets a river,
a boat at hand to sail downstream.
You will appear ahead
at the end of the long road
cutting across chasms,
tall wishes and longings—
the patriarch will decree
denials that will smother
visions of flames dancing
feverishly in the wind.
When you appear alone
at the lone end of the road,
the river dry, boat wrecked
and no foreknowledge
from a retouched picture,
I will surely recognize you:
the one in the bright of night
and mist of day played
moon and sun before me.

(December 9 – 10, 2000)

The Suitor Is Dancing

The suitor is dancing round a tree whose branch
harbours bird and nest he wants on his palm—
he implores the tree to nod its crowned head
and deliver the bird without fright onto his hands.
Now he wears a priest's cloak of white smoke,
the burnt offering whirls like wind dancing in circles.
He spews songs like decrees of a demented dictator
he knew from ministering to mocking victims—
they follow suit without a mind of their own.
Dizzy from dancing, the suitor twists and turns
a traveller rounding the same spot without stop—
the world is spinning on its terra cotta head
& no knowing where and when it will crash.
The smoke shows no sign from above, but its
rings whirl upwards; a compulsive leap of faith.
The suitor pursues, he chants to clear his way—
shall he cross the sea of deep water, or drown
in the bosom of a silt-filled lake and lose sight
of horizons? The bird watches the tree shake,
its body warms up to the dance but isn't sure
of the first step; others look to follow close.
The bird seeks a calm to deliver its token:
a flower already grows from its long beak.
What will exchange for a stalk of flower
from the sweating palm of the suitor?
The bird is a half-dark cloud above the eyes—
the suitor is encumbered by numberless prayers,
the spider's expressway cannot carry him further;
he looks to the sky, faces the east with closed eyes.
He foresees the cloud floating a mountain of cotton.
He makes a jump to be borne along with it—if it
won't come down with prayers, then join it!—
but he comes down hard on the soil. Awake!

(January 26, 2001)

Swimmer

Diving into
the Red Sea
at sunset,
there are corals
to harvest
in deep water.
But will they
make up for
the full moon
walking
on a beach
of cowries?

(January 26, 2001)

Moon Phase

Before the moon phases out its presence
& jeremiads of tears crash dikes of dark,
homegirls hold their breasts erect and high—
they flaunt their banners in the night light,
stick out slit iguana tongues for kisses.

In droves the suitors are coming prepared,
their king an affront to courage; but that
spurs him to cover with a shining body.
There's always one heart that bleeds
in libation to the earth, one log around
to bring back the dying hearth to light.

There are gestures that grow into signatures,
blisters that eat deep to ulcerate the flesh—
the moon is smudged with storm clouds
that will abort the millennial livery of sand.
The homegirls are waiting for suitors
singing their way into town without light!

To My Realist Friend

To the realist
the bird is trussed and thrust on the table,
a dish spiced to fill the appetite.
To the dreamer
the bird is a messenger of the gods
to the world to deliver beauty and love.

You would ask:
can the bird sing its throat dry,
deliver its message of the gods
and still garnish the dinner table?
And I ask back:
if I give you a flower,
will you hold to it long enough
to remember the colour and aroma
that make it infirmary for heartaches?

What do you remember,
or choose to cast away?
Memory of flaming feathers
features in my mind's chamber—
the song wakes the man in me
to dance along a narrow street
to build a nest of words for the swallow.

Shall we wake, the moon gone,
throw thrash at the other—belie
the shower of praise chants?

(February 7, 2001)

Airspace

Now the butterfly enters the fray
and brags about flowery beauty.
It flies too. Still, it's not a bird
and follows the fate of the moth—
a powdery body when touched,
it disintegrates to foul the airspace.

Which colours last and stay fast
in the wind carrying wings aloft?
The sun rises and sets gracefully,
it blazes from one end to another.
I won't choose gold over bronze
in the weaponry offered me
to defend the kingdom of songs,
nor promote white over black
in the race to capture a butterfly
or embrace the rainbow's arms.

The chameleon goes to the market
overflowing with wares and women
and there tries on every hue of brocade—
there he is king of strangers because
of the generous wardrobe of magic.
At home he lies on a bed of dry leaves
and wears a wan coat, a pauper!

My bird dons a bevy of deep colours
to outlast the flash of competitors—
the iroko is not scared of drought,
it won't lose its rich robes to robbers!
From the crown of the tall evergreen,
my bird sings a savoury abundance.

(February 5, 2001)

Healing Song

Today I offer you the healing song
that raises the fowl from its broken legs,
releases the deer from its wound into the wilds
& turns the disabled bee to work on its wings.

I fill the song with draughts of miracle herbs—
take as many deep breaths in your wakeful hours
& at night, as guest of sleep, you will travel far
to leave behind for good stifling discomfort.

It's true that sickness cannot be shared
like a bundle that can be split among friends;
but you can be relieved and cured with love.
I offer this song with all the balm of my soul.

Virulent the current, the calabash drowns not;
the water-lily dances on top of turbulence.
Let the field flame with blood, the warrior
will cut his way home; a victorious chief.

Think of your love and let the blood warm up.
The world smiles and shares out blessings—
the correspondence raises from bed to street!
Today I offer you only the healing song.

(February 3-4, 2001)

Island Residence

Lifted of mists, the island bristles with smiles—
the fishermen break their hooks and throw baits
at fish gurgling beside their waiting dugouts;
they know hunger needs more than fish to fill.

> I am praying for those who went away
> to return with tidal waves—
> it's already darkening
> & islanders have sighted a monster,
> head without body, for a split second.
> The bones that deck the beach at dawn
> come from who did not return the call.

Come, bo; no be here dey say
Mami Wata de baf for full moon?
I fit see am naked and marry am.
The only thing be say, I de fear
the snake e de wear for im body;
but I hear say e de comot am when e de baf—
she no trust am reach make e stand by:
her breasts de stand up for water;
for her bottom, na only God know
wetin de down there man no de see.
I pray God give me luck to see am.
I go use her long hair wen be like black belt
tie am and me together tight for waist.

Mammy Water, row me a boatload of fortune;
dock at the heart you have hurt with longing.
The island brims with boats that ferry to safety,
but ashore strange gods assemble to frolic
and bless wandering souls of wrecked sailors.

    Grandma Amreghe forewarned:
        Don't dive into deep water
        because it mirrors white sand;
        the Ethiope beckons swimmers
        to kiss the star-eyed water maid,
        and she's a deep one to catch
        or follow home—no buttocks
        to flaunt at you; only a fish tail!

I am not going to leave the bird alone, not going
to bargain out the island for a waterless hole.
I need water to cool the body; I plunge in
even as bones smooth as rocks wash ashore.

        Grandma, you gave me the heart
        to take on the monster on my way
        to the bride beaming with smiles
        hiding for me to walk straight into.
        She's so far away; I am still going!

The net is cast into the vast blue—
there's no fishing today in the island;
my hunger is filled with a birdsong.
I don't want to be blinded by visions
of a flaring face mounted on scales.
It's already dawn; my boat still tied.
I give up the deep until the tides
return with the sea's secret message,
misted carriage of corals or cowries!

(February 9, 2001)

Roaming the Lightscape

Cocooned in a circle of light, this night
the moon glows and glares with ample stare.
Beside, a masked man wielding an axe—
human guard or jealous spouse of a beauty,
he follows her as of right her favourite one.

I pace up and down the lightscape, roaming
the sky for an audience with her majesty.
Blacksmith among the stars I am busy
blowing the bellows to blaze the skyline,
positioned to flare my face for recognition.

I keep on playing the villain, praying
for my rival to slip as I wait to spring
forward to take over the bride of light
and share the circle that shines outside
but whose inside nobody really knows.

This night the galaxies debate my fate
without asking for advice from the earth.
I sing of the moon and stars that incorporate
my consuming desires into their lucent
faces.
I pace up and down the lightscape, roaming.

(March 8, 2001)

You Defy Capture

You defy capture by the Canon camera
that sees through seas to the antipodes—
a reel of blank films remains; blotted out,
you mock the magician's conjuring craft.
You hear the call but answer not to escape
the sorcerer's cage, a prize in his chamber.
Spirit, you cannot be caught by iron traps
though you cross the roads of the world.
Wind, you cannot be held by force of arms.

At night you pass for star or full moon,
radiant but too distant to bring down;
at dawn you are wrapped in cool vapours,
staying as long as the sun's fancy allows
when you disappear into a leering voice.
Do you plunge into water so deep, or
transmigrate into one of a hundred birds?
You defy every word the tongue offers
flavoured with favoured eastern aromas;
there's no alphabet to describe your face.

***

If I should paste every face I have seen on
a canvas, what postcards would stare at me!
But how could I tell the so many strangers
in ordinary cotton from divinities come down?
There is always two of a kind, mystics say,
and I must have seen the bird of the east
without a tag to betray the masked body.
The voice I hear from across the world
must come from the muse that declines
recognition—the ultimate modesty—
and I am not going to force the issue.
I know what I do not see staring at me!

***

To the faithful, belief is all it takes.
Somewhere there are ladders to the sky.
The moon is the favourite daughter of God—
I can't get too close without a blinding flash.
I pass Jesus in the street without knowing,
but I know I receive the help I ask for.
The vision of the moon as a boat of light
sucked into the mouth of a mountain wave
confirms the virtue of the sea's beauty.
The sea and sky bring me hidden joy.
Drowning is salvation by water—
to the faithful, belief is all it takes.

***

I dreamt of falling in love with God's daughter.
The muse came my way with another name.

(February 16, 2001)

Ten Pieces

1

Your sun rises before I go to bed.
I see the full moon glistening.
I have not spent a day without smiles.

2

You wear light green
over an overcast sky.
The banana is ripe.

3

On both sides of the road you pass
trees stand transfixed with crossed leaves.
There is no question of your noble birth.

4

A light rain falls over me.
The sun is shining overhead.
I sing for you with a toothache.

5

The harmattan arrives
at a sparkling hearth—
strangers love comfort.

6

You brought heat waves and cool springs,
raised a river of sweat for so much abundance.
You are the demanding god I love to worship.

7

Mist falls all over the forest.
The bird won't perch anywhere now.
I applaud your staying power in space.

8

The island is always breezy.
Maids fan the seated bride.
Others wipe the celebrant's sweat.

9

The green field is growing smaller.
I sing praises of my beautiful totem.
We look to the sky for an answer.

10

The bird flaps arms to leave the east.
A blackout looms across the way.
A new sun rises to steer the flight.

(February 17-18, 2001)

Birdsong

I

Memory, take me to the wetlands
of the beginning, loyal providers;
take me to crosscurrents of the delta
that unite creeks to the deep-minded sea;
let me dip into the herb-dark waters.
I want my voice to flow as a full river
whose currents ripple through the body
to challenge the soul with great depths.

II

Traversing the vast universe,
I wear my favourite's feather—
the parrot's staying power in the sky
carries it across mountains and oceans!
Let me arrive, a welcome guest.

III

I listen to the bird singing
from the flagpole of the forest—
the lavender voice dissolves into the air
I must breathe in and out to live.
Cry out your voice, bird, from the shadows—
the hidden vision taunts me to fly
and knock out the awful distance
that separates spirit from body.
Bird who speaks to the wanderer
just waking to the world of faith,
the alphabet of your language appears
& I join word to word, note to note,
to rise from the blank hole into
the pageantry of colours and flavours.

IV

From the kingdom of green foliage,
you maintain the godly wealth of freshness.
There you see through the rack of the heart
that beats a frantic drum for your majesty.
The pilgrimage has brought me to the farthest,
I have crossed oceans to the eastern seashore
to be in your presence, glowing from mist.
You are the miracle and the magic of light,
the vision and the mission that stir the veins.
I have stepped over the threshold of portals,
I am filled with the ample light you shed,
and begin to see through the mist the bird.

V

I seek happiness for the rest of the journey.
I throw three coins into the fountain, where
my bird dips feathers to deepen their colours
and sips draughts that fill melodies with flavours.
The flight ahead will be straight to the point,
the gods breathe winds to steer the wings
to overfly the red zones of wicked djinns.
Let every perch be on hospitable ground
where there will be ululation for the bride—
my bird is a bride of the entire universe,
welcomed by strangers, family and friends.
Let me reach the farthest on wings of one
whose fate of feathers touches mine.
I throw three coins into the fountain,
seeking happiness upon happiness.

(NYC-Charlotte. February 22-25, 2001)

> But the gods give to mortals not
> everything at the same time.
>
> —Homer, *The Iliad*

Following the Minstrel's Trail

I grew up knowing a musician as a magician.
Paul* captured us from playground or home
into his compound thrown open by bugles—
we called him Ikpugbu, the wonder of our world;
he was a lord to whom we fell captive with delight.

Now a renowned singer boasts he won't open
his mouth until people lend him all their ears.
No, I tell him; the waves of the song should
drown the clattering of the far-flung crowd.
Sing well to yourself, friend, and you will
wake someone from the depths of slumber.
Many folks in a flash abandon their chores
to follow the piper's trail from the floodgate.

When pangs prick the tongue of the singer,
the howl tears through to wake the dumb!
So many live the blues, laugh and cry out
alone in bed at night tossing and turning.
O god of rippling melodies, great dispenser,
stop my restive tongue but not with affliction
until the dark clouds gathering strength
break out a deluge of flavoured songs.

(January 17, 2001)

---

* Paul Orovwigho of Okurekpo, my elementary school teacher, great singer and performer.

Many Lives

I get scared
when I foresee drought
with its undertaker company
of roaming fires and dunes.
Fortunately so far
a hurricane season
always breaks in
to sustain my faith.

My Father's Eyes

When my father lost his right eye
to what modern medicine told me was
glaucoma, cataract, or some other name,
that did not diminish his vision of the world
he knew to be swamped with hostility.
Ever alert to what came from any side,
he smiled heartily to everybody in town
even as witches gloated over his careless acts
that helped them triumph in senseless rivalries.
The remaining eye did not leave him anxious
in hunting expeditions or games of hide-and-seek.
He always closed eyes anyway to confirm facts.
Fiction, for that matter, hadn't been born.
It took the look-alike of endless sleep, death,
to rob the visionary of details of contours—
he followed the map he once drew clearly with
both eyes into the freeway of blank horizons.
Science blindfolded my father into a pit
covered with herbs and barks, but
the world he didn't know still lives
on the fiction and fact of his fatherhood.

(Warri. May, 2000)

Blues

I

I am the tortoise stuck to
a charm-bearing fruit-plant,
bound to be caught and
stripped in the marketplace.
I have become handicapped
from fighting to free myself—
hands and feet, head and trunk
all stuck; the exhibit waits.

II

Let me be
the sunbird
singing blues,
even as others
desirous of my plumes
take aim at my colours.
I sing in the bush
flushed with sunlight,
a twig in my mouth.

Entering the New Millenium

The millipede arrives at a way station
without losing one of its thousand legs.
And that raises a mammoth applause
and bonfires that will piecemeal consume
a century whose ripeness is everybody's fear.
The snake lost its tail and grew a second head!
We prepare for the wake of a worrisome warrior
whose offspring boasts of breaking his record.
If we celebrate the hatching of toxic eggs,
we must prepare against poisonous birds
whose droppings will burn the air we breathe.
Is arrival all, after the elephant trampled farms?
Is waking all, after dynasties of nightmares?
The world vibrates with cannons and carnivals
because the millipede arrives at a way station
without losing one of its thousand legs
though a dark mushroom hangs overhead.

I Want to Dance

*(after Eloho's statement and dance
at the Comfort Suites)*

With Papa Wemba's flavoured voice
pulling everybody off their seats,
the spirit of the dance possessed her.
"I want to dance!" she cried out,
steering wheelchair to the dance floor.
Strapped, she threw hands, then head,
from one direction to another—
she trembled, gesturing. Limbs
for long atrophied from thieving
strokes and comatose cells wake.
"I want to dance!" and she got
not one partner but many, dazed—
Mom danced with her, as others
and I that she had cast a spell over.
The floor shook harder with her entry,
head and hands dancing for coy legs;
the wheelchair holding back her eyes
from fully lighting into magic stars.
And so she danced, hands uplifted
and head nodding frantically to
cadences; a worshipping priestess.
She danced to life, despite the strap.
"I want to dance!" Who won't?

(June 21, 2000)

Four Pieces

I

When day broke
on the Niger, the Delta
still disrobed and bleeding—
the robbers had neither removed
all the loot nor sheathed daggers.
But the cry of the wounded
stifled by massive storms
drew a column of silence.
Her jewelry of honour
sold to stave off drought
in their inland capital.
The Delta bleeds; disrobed.

II

The harmattan breezed in
with a scythe, not net or hook,
to fish Delta rivers and creeks.
Within seven days of
            its prowling,
the water turned cold
            and blood-toned.

E-e Ogiso!
Ogiso!
E-e Ogiso!

III

In the General's office
a master plan
to bridge the entire length
of the Niger River and creeks.
He will conscript fishers
to nail their own coffins!

IV

Those who laughed with a slice
of our coconut cake in their mouths
still spat at our backs—we could read
the mean minds of who smiled at us,
hiding our brides among their harems.
We had no friends among the powers.
They introduced a bill to move the lower
Niger and creeks from the abode of arbor
to throw enough green over desert dust.
We'd see how soon moonshine tries
so hard to dry a deluge of high storms!

In the Water World

The egg of a crocodile
mauls a mudfish with fear—
the family of fins knows too well
what the shadow embodies.

A curious waterfowl hatches
the abandoned eggs of a crocodile—
it will learn in a matter of minutes
to take to the air and land far.

Once the cock opens the door
for dawn to set out
to map the empire of light,
the shadow loses its body.

And after the journey's done
and a dark net covers horizons,
eyes shut before the naked emperor
& there's no use for masks.

In the water world,
as in other worlds,
we hear of the likes of
mudfish and waterfowl

empowering crocodiles.

The Apprentice

After apprenticeship—
in his first outing—
a young hunter looked out
more than eager to shock
with a prize game.
A brush stirred ahead
& he instantly took aim,
fingers on the trigger.
But in a flash a veteran
seized his feverish arm:
"Not so fast. Never fire
at what you don't see!"
To everybody's relief,
a snake-bitten boy
hurled himself out of
a broken ring of beaters
in place of the game
the young hunter wanted
to pluck as his first prize.

Reflections

Around
the corner,
what the hand
cannot reach
to avoid
a glitch.

***

Longer
by just
an inch,
the piece
that needs
to snap in
and turn on
the circle
but cannot
be mended
without
wrecking
the whole.

***

The plantain
whose leaf
covers
from rain
ripens
in
dry seasons.

***

Power is
not measured
by loud ranting.
The silent one
whose patience
breaks records
can also laugh
hilariously.

***

A giant's shadow
more than
covers
with awe
the entire
neighbourhood
from snipers.

(August 8, 2000)

Three Mami Wata Poems

1

From deep water
the calm guest
whose cleanliness
defies human soil
& yet blood and flesh
divinely sculpted,
so smooth and cool.
Jet locks gathered
into a crown—
a caste of gold
in charcoal country.
She moves in
and out of water
without ripples,
all stars pale
in her presence.
Desired bride no
groom dares share
her bed-chamber,
a python beside her.
She throws herself
at men she wants to
castrate and cast away.
From deep water
the calm guest
so clean, and
on land surreal.

2

Mami Wata falls
into deep water, and
strangers to her craft
scramble to save her
from drowning and dying!
And they dive straight into
a riverbed of white sand
whose mirrors shatter
their round lives. Then
Mami Wata reappears,
unruffled by the clamour
and murmur of mourners.
She glistens more than ever.

3

If Mami Wata makes a home
of your island, present her
bouquets of proud flowers; but
beware of the turbulence around,
for she surrounds herself
with swirls, swirls and swirls.
You will have to abandon
your only foothold to her
whose constant love flares
leave no one from smothering,
except to dive deep for cover.
Throwing yourself at sharks
bristling underwater saves
no fugitive of discomfort
from disfiguring death ahead.
Mami Wata and sharks after you,
the island melts into deep water.

(Port Jefferson, NY. August 12, 2000)

To My Feminist Friend

With barbed words, you smacked
the goddess of all the nubile girls;
you revered no full-breasted tyrant
who sold women's pleasures to men.
You wore no livery of Sowei, whose
Sande league of initiates capitulated
before petty patriarchs—slaves or
spouses, their sharing made no sense.
At school you were leader of boys.
You feared rivers, raced across bridges—
you did not want to meet water spirits,
though you would have loved to swim.
Today a feminist professor, you wear
white attire to party; not body marked
with kaolin for excision by midwives
whose home knives flared with zeal
to disable girls before erect boys.
From adolescence you shook your
right forefinger at the female mask
that blindfolded women into a hole.
You are the new leader of the girls.

A Child Holds the Lamp

(for Adama, after reading her "Misbah")

So, the watch continues as it has
from its man-begotten beginning.
Imbecile thought that a child
should hold a lamp after an adult!
The lamp burns, night still covers
in folds of darkness; it clears not.
The child knows not yet her charge;
she feels not the pulsating rhythms
pulling the pot headlong to the spring;
she's just too young to hear loud
the feverish panting of the starved
one crying for waiting communion.
She knows not why ripe fruits pray
to be plucked or fall fast in a breeze.
She holds the lamp all right, but does
she see the shadow that envelops
the adult charge in seek-and-hide?
She shares in the tokens of love, but
does she know respite from prison;
can she see twofold in a dark cloud?
Who doesn't know that harmattan cold
drives hard to seek a sparkling hearth?
Let the watch continue! As expected,
she will wrap herself around at night
whose light blights in a cloud or hole.
The lamp liberates—cools the heart!
Such imbecile thought that a child's eye
should see through the dark of the heart!

(Maiduguri-Warri. December 20 – 22, 2000)

Guest of the Forest

The forest laid out a feast; an evergreen canopy overhead—
from horizon to horizon the abundance stretched the eyes
& by the roadside we stopped to partake of the communion.
It was in the late afternoon; nobody else except a wine-girl
entered the breezy fold of the generous shawl of deep green.
The rest of the world cruised past, always in a hurry.
Beside the mat of leaves thrown upon the dark soil,
beside the tall populace of rubber, palms, and others
sat water-resisting bamboo benches for us pilgrims.
Here all faiths of the land congregate to toast peace
and love over sectarian suspicions and bad blood.
We knew here was neither Jerusalem nor Mecca,
we came not to chant dirges of distant prophets.
The queen of the plains and clearings took a stroll
deep into the forest side by side with the homeboy;
her veil thrown out—whom do you cover from
in the pungent ruts of deer, porcupine, and warthog?
I started a game of hide-and-seek to taunt her fearful
of the forest, but spontaneous laughter broke out
& we gave ourselves up. We raced back through
burrs and goat paths to the bamboo joint away.
She was as scared by snakes as I—none slid by.
The wine-girl had readied the table, set with
bottles of palm-wine and huge goblets by the side.
To the earth first, the share of worthy ancestors;
then to the host of parched but absent beggars!
Wine freshly tapped and emptied of the palm
in the day's second shift, the tongue rolled
reluctant to funnel draughts down the throat
eagerly lavishing savories of the cool spring.
The tapster knew the trade, his trees so blessed—
who would not defy death to seek his return,
should he fall down and breach the luxury?
Foam stuck to the lips—I teased her who wore
a beard; I played the clown of white-painted lips.

She gloated over bending to breaking point
the teetotaler's resolve with draughts of pleasure—
I didn't hold back; she had earlier broken the fast.
The forest lost its fright in the night that came;
the pilgrims on benches above a mat of leaves
wallowing in a cool breeze, abandoned by the girl
who had asked for no price for this feast of the forest.
Should we have followed the many ruts to dwelling
places, or sat as we did at the threshold of beast
and man and enjoy the trance while it lasted
before starting sentry duty for faithless factions?
It was Christmas and Id el Kabir, a double whopper!
O guest of the forest, queen of plains and clearings,
carry away this cornucopia of a hospitable day
and tell the story of the forest to the grassland.

(January 21-23, 2001)

Signaling Drums

The women who conceived the night of the hyena
are coming to term in the vicinity of the snake

they have crossed a mountain village without gates
for long evacuated into the bowels of a monster rock

they no longer count the new moons on their way
for fear of overstaying their days of good luck

they have borne their loads with an innocent face
they do not look back to pick what fell from them

the market is still far away from the produce
they must buy to nurse the foetus into a wonder child.

Murmuring drums signal the appearance
of hope trembling before an iron gate.

(Okigbo, excuse my forays into labyrinths
where only the insane come back safe)

And there's been the quandary of the spectacle
of the chameleon that the tortoise cannot fathom

& so falls into the abyss of entrapment.
Do not dance to the drums of spirits—

they beat them to assemble for a feast
& that's the last call for a human to obey

there's no threshold to cross into the congress
but every movement is a denial of body life.

Will forward steps thrust into a moon
dressed in glistening linen covering scars?

The hyena now parties all night with the snake
the distant drums keep the market from flowing.

The women are scared to death at sundown
by rumblings in their bellies thundering harmattan

with midwives transfixed by sorcerers their lovers
handicapped from attending to their labour cries

they deliver babies laughing at their own deformities
the snakes are poised to bite off what they cannot swallow

no one will escape the storm of tears gathering strength
in the season of mourning fear death by drowning.

Not all drums are meant for dancing
& there will be no naming the unnamable...

(Reno, NV. February 9, 2002)

Tobi

I had to come out to relieve myself
this bone-chilling morning, and behold
whom did I see out that early?
It was Tobi, the rich one who sleeps
when everybody else is out working!
The toad was out, and I knew
some break-in had gone on somewhere.
It had taken him longer than planned.
Panting and dishevelled, he brandished
a torch before me to cover the misdeed.
He was not coming from farm at dawn;
he had never set hooks in the stream, and
it was the wrong season anyway, so dry.
About five minutes after he breezed past,
a crowd of neighbouring villagers stormed in—
they followed the right trail, knew the thief's
body odour and headed straight for his door.
I am happy outsiders know the thief among us.
I heard later he closed his eyes and snored
loud;
but they knew his trick—he was still sweating
from the race for his life through the night.
What else made him sweat in frosty dawn?
They dragged him out to the marketplace.
There, let him dance to the drum he beats.
Who pities the thief who boasts of wealth?

Anthill Residence

"The bird that quarrels with the ground but perches on the anthill forgets that the anthill is still earth" (Bini proverb and subject of Bruce Onobrakpeya's artwork titled "Ulelefe").

They took flight of the ground for the anthill
they abandoned the earthen floor for the rooftop
they left Lagos for New York.

The ground rubs itself with mud
the land paints its face with ochre
Abibiman stinks from daily dirt.

The anthill wears a made-up face
the anthill tones up its skin to glow
America wears high heels over the mess on the floor.

They are more muscular than ever
they are thinner and taller than ever
they are millionaires by conversion.

From the hill they look down on the ground
that still wears mud on its face
and rolls on the vomit of its voracious head.

The anthill provides exceptional height
safe are those who camp on the hill
they don't struggle to have the upper hand.

The higher they live the cooler the breeze they breathe
the farther from the ground the freer their lives
they eat and wipe their mouths with table cloths.

They close their eyes to the scum of the anthill's armpit
they are deaf to gunshots in the rap that drowns street cries
they gasp for air in the entombed paradise of their flight.

They lose their tongues from violent kisses
they exhaust themselves to please sex partners
they are possessed with their new loves.

When they abused its gods, the ground threatened them
they are hurt by the anthill and swallow their phlegm
up there they cannot exercise their rightful tongues.

They used to cry in the marketplace over the ground's hurt
now they cry at night in bed over the anthill's bruises
nobody wipes their tears but themselves,

There's tolerance of the ground because of its oil
there's adoration of the anthill because of its height
these relatives have forgotten what binds them

The ground is hell but the anthill's not paradise
the anthill's high but nowhere the sky
the ground and the anthill are one uneven earth.

Night

If I listened to others, I would look you
in the eye and spit at your face. But you
are no worse offender than your accusers.
You have had your share of bad company,
but should not be the carrier and the sacrifice.
Some of your stars are so faint they disappoint.
Others brilliant beauties, we build them shrines.
Look at the moon when full and you will be
dazzled and launched high into another orbit.

I do not need to go out to understand
those with attitude—I have lived
in the South, breaking colour bars
because I am dark; it's a lifelong task.

There's barely a career without highs and lows,
and you have had quite a number of swings.
You are not robber, rapist, or murderer
but are derided for covering up for them;
none remembers the refuge you provide.
Imagine if there was no reprieve from the sun!
I sing your praise for freeing people from
islet homes to company lovers everywhere.

Night,
    heal my wounds with starlight
    raise my voice with your silence
    wash my soles with waves of dew
    lift my heart to the highest clouds
    freshen me with your sea-breeze
    save me in your vassal forest.

In your sun-screened dominion, Night,
I lay down my bull offering.
Take over bundles that crush the back.
Keep me in your swathe of melanin,

rock me to sleep and to wake strong.
I have had enough of daylight
that blurs vision within.
Night, I need you as I need love.
Without you there's no morning.

> It is because I ate another fruit that I know *duriak* is better than melon.
> —Taban lo Liyong, *Homage to Onyame*

> We must graze where we are tied.
> —Edwidge Danticat, *Breath, Eye and Memory*

From This Soil That Hurts

From this soil that hurts so deep
with blades of grass and tripping stumps

that the body half-dies from exhaustion,
smarting heat that scalds the body

comes the salt that gives savour
to the tongue; the crop that enlivens—

there's no refuge not built out of fear,
no steadfastness in drifting aimlessly.

O soil that threatens damnation
and yet saves from the fiercest army,

for fifty-three years you have held me,
for decades kept me safe in labyrinths

you smacked me like a baby needing direction;
stroked me with warm but hard palms of love.

Can I weep tears of joy for this hurt, annul
the saga of anguish with the stream of salt

be bonded to the god of democracy
whose scars of freedom I must wear

to range freely a citizen of the nation
and not of a mere paper constitution

where demands of a native son
keep me captive of wild traditions?

I live with everybody's envied blessing,
a curse nobody acknowledges for once.

An enduring marriage keeps secrets of love
that thrills and aches at the same time

like this soil I always come back to
to smudge with soles and knees even as

it hurts deep, the salt that sustains me
while I wash off its brown stains.

***

Every crop, fruit, and vegetable of the soil
smacks the tongue with a heartwarming tang

the ineluctable savour moistens desire
for more; hence the minstrel eats voraciously

for the deep song that only the home breath
can raise effortlessly from daily communion.

(Warri. December 13-14, 2001)

Women Writing Africa, in Fez

"Where are the women?" asked
Tuzyline, discovering herself
alone in a thronged file of aliens.
Her kinswomen had disappeared
in a flash of silent retreat.
Men are incapable of stealth—
barbarians, they had arrived
with loud reports of cannon.

The women's league revise griots' songs,
they write Africa on volumes of finery
they wore for centuries with deep hurt.
Now they suppress fright, as they do
who must fight through barricades
to seize back their robbed treasures.

The Amazons withdrew to the bathroom
where mirrors offer a last chance of revision
before the exhibition about to hit the road.
As spirits of masks reside in the wood,
so do women's power in bodies that men
crave to embrace to prove their courage.

At the hotel counter, men change fat bills
before journeying to the ruins of earlier powers
that women must have laid flat—what empire
on earth of men is not vulnerable to herstory?
Nobody computes the inhuman cost of conquest!
Battered, Volubilis remains a postcard beauty.

The women sing seductively to invoke a stream
to drown men who after feasts forsook them
to their wits, shells, scarves and tears—
as usual, the patriarchs deflect poisoned arrows
by stoppering their ears with the very cotton
the women prepared in lone hours of anticipation.
The mirror exercises no charm over the blind!

What are men doing that drive women from
the file that leads to the exchange counter?
Why are flowers not always sunlit in their seasons;
why are hunters deaf to the antelope's cry;
where are the women whose rooms are vacant?
And what men are hearty when crushed
with fat bills, possessing but dispossessed?

(March 15-21, 1999)

Jack London

In the wine
country of Sonoma
another meteor
burnt itself out.
Incandescent
the Valley of the Moon
glows with memory
of the casualty
whose blaze fills
books and state park
despite ashes
beneath a stone.

Walla Walla

Some land-locked folks
after a pact with fate
to make a desert
grow abundance
built a homeland.

They learnt fast that
only through magic
wrought by soiled
and sweating hands
can the handicapped
survive adversities.

The land carries
a scabbed face,
but in it God's grains
through constant toil
transform in the sun
into a green sheet.

Here sun-wrenched days
eternally drenched
with water-spouts;
below the crusted face
waters, *walla walla*.

And so in this haven
distanced from marauders,
the peace-gened ones
reap a windfall
that shocks a laughter-
prone world.

The Size of Manhood

(on the London-Edinburgh Express)

Let nought be wasted.
They learnt from birth
the frugal science of ants,
a habit of industry.
Since God denied them
abundance of land
and not of mind,
they stretched the isle
into a big world.
With hedges as safe
guards against feuds,
they partitioned their
lot into a draft board
from which extract
their fill with self-
satisfying pride.
Do you wonder why
landless children
"ruled the waves"?
Hunger to grow big!
Do you blame the rat
for tying up elephants
of Africa and India
by whatever spell
and looting wealth
to prop itself into
a world power? Man
hood has nothing
to do with mere size.
If it had, of course,
impotent giants
wouldn't be legion.

More Italian Than Catholic

I expected domed cathedrals,
frescos and flocks of saints
to delight my wayward eyes.
What could be more Italian
than a Roman Catholic garb?
I had braced myself for
a kidnap-free sojourn, with
neither name nor millions
of lira to tempt the south-
poised Mafia. I knew that
Romans ruled the world
of old history books, and
Petrarch and Michelangelo
their adored wizards...

Now in the lake region,
pre-Alpine every inch,
I see so many people
with mindful hands
cut their own course
out of austere rocks.
They tunnel stone
into highways; with
persistent perspiration
till mountains to yield
barns of abundance.

They scale the sky with
cable cars—the abysmal
slope would scare life
out of a stunt demon.
They so measure out
the lake-possessed land
that nowhere lies idle
from loving care.

My quarrel had been
that the land bred
the Beast.* I now
know they hanged
him heels down
to exorcise the evil
in their heavy hearts.
I take home a camera
load of exposure
to sell this vision.

---

* The Beast: Benito Mussolini, fascist leader.

Rivera's Brush

*(after seeing Diego Rivera's paintings
on the National Palace walls in Mexico City)*

1

As elsewhere, the gun conferred lordship on conquistadors.
They stamped the cross on foreheads that knew a kinder God,
built churches atop revered temples of born mystics—
they believed spirits of native gods would disappear
from the weighty discomfort of being sat on the head.
And they were wrong, those who trusted only guns!

2

You can humour history with a footnote.

"Thanks to the black slave Juan Garrido:
he brought three different grains
to benefit the New World."
Such the belated compliment of the conquistador,
who brandished the gun for civilization;
such the rabid rat's blowing the very wound
it had inflicted upon its over-generous host!

"Thanks to the black slave Juan Garrido."
Yet they shackled the Guinean to do their bidding!
That's why, with a brush of wizardry,
Rivera captured the robot of Juan Garrido
and the riot of beasts, conquerors.

Diego, conquistadors entered your watercolour
and came out their true selves.
But over the deathfield of mass humiliation,
the eagle and feathered serpent look out
beyond the veneer of whitewash
into temples of true gods,
into sun and moon returning
with resplendence.

Santa Maria

Gliding above glittering water,
moon ablaze and showering
gold dust on a blue canvas,
the cockpit announces:
"Get ready for landing
    at Santa Maria, the Azores."
Belts fastened, headrest upright,
the wizard bird flexes wings,
tests its land-perching craft.
Santa Maria, one of nine islets
that compel love at first sight,
will hold me and others
for an hour of refueling.
Sitting on the tarmac at Santa
Maria—Azores—Portugal,
my eyes suddenly open to
ships that hauled kinsfolk
into steel nets of the West.
I think of them conquistadors
flaunting papal asientos
to covet the fortune of others.
Does Holy Mary immaculate
deserve the cross inflicted
on her body by Portugal?
This glory of the earth wilts
into a historical wilderness
engulfing Elmina, Abomey,
Benin, Calabar, and Luanda.
Holy Mary praying for us,
understand why I curse.
Time passes, memory remains.
As I lift off, I think of freedom
and the smoking god of the gun.
I still curse in the name of God.

Discovering Lands

I
(Bucharest)

When the steel-feathered one
perched at Otopeni, they clapped
the applause I had heard in Lagos
when Nigeria's flying elephant
touched down without any hurt.
We milled down stairs, not
through chutes as in Heathrow,
Kennedy or Charles de Gaulle,
into a bus in the flaming air.
Gypsies sleeping on the floor
welcomed me to the lounge;
then a class of orphans tearing
sandwich from their teacher
eyeing the first Okpara man
they might have ever seen.
Dracula postcards invited me
to send a message home
about my longest transfer,
killing time with exploration.
With fellow strangers from India
and China compared our lands'
separate heartaches—too many
poor, too few rich; robbers!
An American animal trainer
impressed with his travels
and open mind, though
he condemned OJ before
the defence told its story.
We drifted through hazes
of Caecescu and the Stazi,
through polite and non-
dissenting guards to

the cafeteria. Choked
with smoke, I cursed all
to whom cigarette was staple.
Nine hours later, I jostled
my way through Jews
blanketing themselves
with bright memories
en route the fabled
land of divine birth.
On lift-off, they again
clapped the applause
as in Lagos thousands
of miles down south.
Caecescu and the Stazi
left their marks as the
uniformed jackals home.

II
(Jerusalem)

Scriptured
black:
messiah dead,
nation born.
The world lives
with leftover light
of a dead star.

***

A desert
green from
faith of sweat.

The Liar

Here's the big liar,
a priest robed in silken faith;
a singer who doesn't open his mouth.
He now says he toured Jerusalem
that everybody knows is in heaven!
After constipating from alien dishes,
he says the beloved stars are dead
when we see them light up every night.
Meet the big liar of the land
no doubt possessed by a strange spirit
saying he walked the Avenue of the Dead
to ascend the peaks of both Sun and Moon.

He must be a big liar,
this child who wears his father's hat as his;
he denies the tree we planted root-up
could not have grown to the huge iroko.
He easily wins the lying contest
who says he is older than his parents,
themselves babies of his generation.
If he were not a big liar,
how could he claim to have climbed
a tree to stand on its leaves?
There he is, the greatest liar,
who says his love has four breasts
when it's known all over that
every woman barely carries two full ones.

Sole emperor of the lying world,
he lies and lies the more he loses
his sight and hearing to imaginings
and the globe contracts into his palm.

Desert Night Shuttle

I didn't expect camel riders or cavalries
thrusting spears through empty spaces—
there had been less theatrical modes of spreading
the faith of multiple ablutions in a watchful world.
I was not carrying gold to barter for salt,
nor seeking arcane scripts to fortify talismans.
Airborne up to a frontier capital and ferried across
a flowing river into unreadable millennia of sand,
I knew I had arrived at last at the ancient land.

My companion moon and stars emblazoned the night
like burnished figures inscribed on a blue canvas—
incarnate smiles of gods, they lit my soul.
I rode in the delegated car of hospitality
toward my host—thank God I insisted
that my son share in the fantasy (and death,
if it came). I am not the one to balk at
invitations to meet strangers in their land;
I, who lifted the elephant with my teeth!
Perhaps a white trimming in the red uniform
that the world's powerful made his straitjacket.
But who knew without seeing him at home?

I envisioned the twin Tigris and Euphrates,
I summoned Nebuchadneza from nebulous lore;
chanted the epic of Gilgamesh (thanks to Aridon).
I foresaw knights lifting belles to their arms.
On the vast body of the sand-smooth beauty,
no war scars or bones to tear my tender eyes—
lives, then carcasses, disposed of by mass burial!
The rumble of flights dead, only falling stars
crashed noiselessly. What beauty, I cried within.

Night throttled us to the rest centre, an oasis—
sparkling water and home-grown fruits and crops;
an underground river surely broke out here.

I relished this stop in the unknown emptiness
with a sigh for my people who in wet lands
have none of this cornucopia of delicacies.
Here I washed off dust, took an express nap
in the cool promise of advancing caravans.

And in Baghdad I arrived at a surreal dawn, misted.
I saw the land, a little more scarred than elsewhere;
saw people human like everywhere, a little more dazed.
I unwrapped my three-piece bundle in expectation
of reading a message to the Emperor of the Sands:
"Warrior ambushed in a desert plain" still breaks through;
"The Earth," the one who doesn't shake with fear
and can carry anything that falls from the skies.
I also had the bird that dips its beak into a lake
and imagines that the water has diminished!
I feared what would be taken for flattery or insult.

For some scare flashed through army ranks,
I missed the window allotted me to shake hands.
The soot-faced guards kept the chieftain out of reach
of strangers of which I was one. No risks tolerated
even from one wielding a printmaker's paraphernalia!
I have for long known that big ones hide underground,
and I surmised he went under concrete for the period.
In his stead a faithful deputy whose face the world knew
took my son and me to witness the unknown wonder
of Baghdad, a cache of invaluable works from the world over.
Who would ever expect the isolated one to have a pet love?
For his lord, the minister purchased my signed pieces
at my price to keep in that ample warehouse of beauty.
What use is beauty entombed, if no dream of uprising?

I shuttled back through the desert's imperial sun
in the eternity of dust. Another rest place, still
a bazaar of fruits and crops not in my wet lands.
This beauty wasn't embargoed by powers from vision,
a tortuous line crafted in a night blazing with effulgence;

caravaned in moon and stars whose bonfires I witnessed.
Was I crazy with exhibition or ambition to journey
that far to wrest from the smarting land green herbs
that would raise a field of abundance at home?
I delivered a message to the warehouse, unsure.
But who sings like me of a desert night shuttle
brings home the promise of a fresh harvest...

Awaiting Sentence

"In darkness, the twilight is still light"
(Sergei Pianzin)

Smoke smothers inside.
Outside a hurricane
snatches the tin roof.
The body endures.
Africa awaits a sentence—
twilight of dawn or dusk,
the silhouette redefines.
The spider bridges on,
the snake makes up its
narrow face under grass.
Shut out or closed in,
it pains either way.
The mind needs shelter
to exercise freedom.
The sunbird still flies
but with broken wings
through half-dark days,
recovering its way home.

The Open Spaces of My Life

You don't enter everywhere that's open—
eyes measure how you can fit in, unbroken,
before you hulk your trunk through the pass.
We would like to be believers in freedom
to practice separate faiths in safe places.
Even storms don't drive people into holes
just because they are open, penetrable—there
are places too dark to enter even when invited.
You look ahead to where you want to be.
The whole year's as open to surprises
as it's locked firmly with familiar bolts.
You can stare at the still life of fruits
and not rid yourself of famine's torture.
I like to wander into what is kept away,
break through dreary frontiers for hope.
The desert's open, but not for me;
unless to start a lavish thunderstorm!

Eyes

They must be watching me:
ancestors from astral towers;
relatives from the top of the family tree;
townsfolk from the main market;
friends from frequent letters;
witches from their coven night-stand;
ladies from photos of opportunity;
passersby from their proximity.

What else will they be up to—
the stars that activate a network of eyes,
the moon that waxes in my heart;
the sun that doesn't set in my day?

They watch my every move
which I must report upon return
even if I implicate myself
to corroborate their multiple visions.
When I put my head in one place,
they already know where my legs would go.
To lie will mean spitting at their faces
& I know the disgrace awaiting the tortoise.

I don't know which is the worse peril:
going bare-handed into the bush
to capture live a leopard
with a chant memorized from the womb,
or these touch-and-go forays
into undiscovered worlds, whose
regions like here rage battlefields.

Wherever I find myself
I see them craning necks
to pry into my whereabouts.
To them I remain the naked child
named Moware by village elders.

I am still on the journey they set me on—
already made Jerusalem; I shall see Ughoton!
It is much farther though than I thought,
I haven't even got to the outskirts of my desire.
I won't shame myself in the task.

When the Migrant Returns Home

When the migrant returns home,
he sings out-of-date songs
to the mockery of stay-at-homes
now envious of his higher height
till he hears fresh tunes
which he adopts into his repertory
to be one voice with home boys.
He has his own dig on stale things
that need outside breeze to freshen
and boasts of the spectacle of vision
that cannot be shared except in tales—
everybody listens to his fantasies
and wishes they happen here.
Only there, the goddesses that
embrace the fortunate traveller.
He sheds borrowed accents—
it's hard for memory
to abandon the refuge
that kept him alive
for the safe return.
Udje music doesn't lose
its edge despite its age
unlike *igoru* and others
it stays in hearts and heads—
it's the native bound to the soil.
Salt eats edges to a new sharpness.
What's in *Catch your Gulder** and *obito***
rhythms that set men and women on fire?
The migrant returns with relief
but confused by cacophonies.

Many friends of youth gone
he retains what's left of knowledge
and makes new ones to cope with
the flood that threatens to drown him.

(Warri. December 15, 2001)

---

* Catch your Gulder: the title of a record by Okpa Arigbo, who plays what has come to be described as Urhobo disco at burial ceremonies and other traditional social occasions in the Niger Delta area of Nigeria.

** Obito is the Pidgin English for "obituary" and is the same dance music type that Catch your Gulder exemplifies.

Glossary

Abibiman: Akan for land of black peoples; here, Africa.
Ananse: Akan for spider that in myth is witty and weaves a thread to the sky for a banquet with God.
Aridon: Urhobo god of memory and muse.
Ethiope: river in Niger Delta area of Nigeria.
Igoru: a type of music in Urhobo areas in the 1940s. Here it is used to represent music that hits the scene and soon falls out of vogue.
Kora: string instrument of the Senegambian area of West Africa.
Mami Wata: mermaid popular in myths of West Africa—fair in complexion, a human face and fish bottom.
misbah: Arabic for lamp.
Ogiso: In Urhobo myths, tyrannical ruler of Benin whose wanton human sacrifices started the exodus of the Urhobo people to their current home in the Niger Delta.
Okpara: town in Delta State of Nigeria and home of the poet.
Olokun: goddess of the sea, wealth, and beauty.
Owena: title for master-artist in Urhobo/Edo.
Sande: female initiation society of the Mende and other groups of Sierra Leone and Liberia.
Sowei: the female leader, an adult, of the Sande group.
Udje: a type of song, poetry and dance performance of the Urhobo people.
Volubilis: Roman town now in ruins in present-day Morocco.
Walla Walla: in the southern part of America's Washington State, a town whose name derives from the Native American word for water and which thus means "land of many waters."

www.ingramcontent.com/pod-product-compliance
Lightning Source LLC
Chambersburg PA
CBHW011743220426
43666CB00017B/2889